HISTORY OF INVENTIONS

Space Exploration

From Rockets to Space Stations

Tracey Kelly

BROWN BEAR BOOKS

Published by Brown Bear Books Ltd

4877 N. Circulo Bujia
Tucson, AZ 85718
USA

and

Unit 1/D, Leroy House
436 Essex Rd
London N1 3QP
UK

ISBN 978-1-78121-456-5 (library bound)
ISBN 978-1-78121-472-5 (paperback)

Library of Congress Cataloging-in-Publication Data available on request

Text: Tracey Kelly
Designer: Supriya Sahai
Design Manager: Keith Davis
Picture Manager: Sophie Mortimer
Editorial Director: Lindsey Lowe
Children's Publisher: Anne O'Daly

Picture Credits

Front Cover: Shutterstock: KK Tan.
iStock: Otto Krause, 4, Shenki, 9; NASA: 6, 10, 13, 14, 18, 21, Apollo Landings, 12, JSC, 19, Kennedy Space Center, 8, Photojournal, 17; Public Domain: 5b, Rijksmuseum, 5tr; Shutterstock: Pavel Chagochkin, 20, Dotted Yeti, 16, travelview, 7; Thinkstock: Dorling Kindersley, 11, 15.
Key: t=top, b=bottom, c=center, l=left, r=right

Brown Bear Books has made every attempt to contact the copyright holder.
If you have any information, please contact: licensing@brownbearbooks.co.uk

Manufactured in the United States of America
CPSIA compliance information: Batch#AG/5624

Websites

The website addresses in this book were valid at the time of going to press. However, it is possible that contents or addresses may change following publication of this book. No responsibility for any such changes can be accepted by the author or the publisher. Readers should be supervised when they access the Internet.

Contents

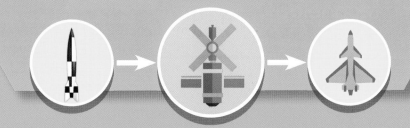

Reaching for the Stars

People have always wanted to fly into space. But they did not always have spacecraft! First, they found ways to make small rockets fire into the air.

Fireworks
The first rockets were fireworks. They were invented in China in the 600s. Fireworks used gunpowder to make an explosion. Modern spacecraft use the same technology.

Fire Arrows

The Chinese used fire arrows as weapons. They shot them into enemy camps. Later, European navies shot fire rockets from ships.

Rocket Man

Stories tell of a Chinese man who tried to go to outer space. That was in the 1500s. He tied 47 fireworks to his chair. His servants lit the fireworks. The fireworks exploded. The man was never seen again!

Read on ... to find out about spacecraft that helped humans visit the Moon and space.

V-2 Rocket

The first rocket had no crew. It was called the V-2. The V-2 was used as a weapon during World War II. This flying bomb first flew in 1942. Later, it was tested for space travel.

Space Monkey
Scientists sent animals into space. Albert II was a monkey. He flew on a V-2. Albert II survived the flight. But he died when the V-2 crash-landed.

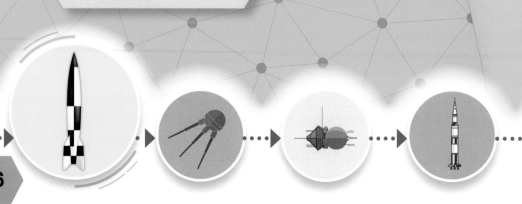

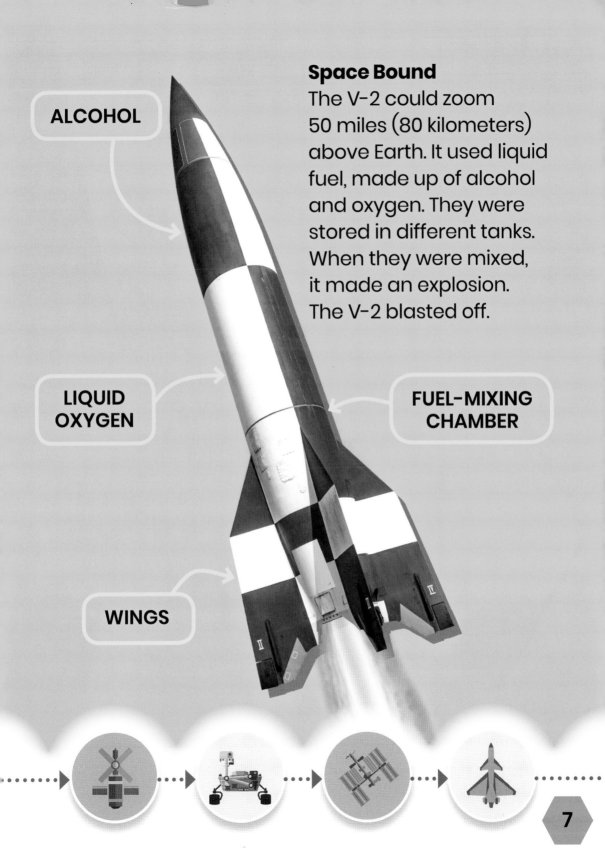

ALCOHOL

Space Bound
The V-2 could zoom 50 miles (80 kilometers) above Earth. It used liquid fuel, made up of alcohol and oxygen. They were stored in different tanks. When they were mixed, it made an explosion. The V-2 blasted off.

LIQUID OXYGEN

FUEL-MIXING CHAMBER

WINGS

Sputnik I

Sputnik I was the first satellite. A satellite is a machine sent into space. Sputnik I was built by the Soviet Union. It stayed in orbit around Earth for three months.

Space Race
Countries raced to get into space. The Soviet Union got there first with Sputnik I. The United States built its first satellite the next year. It was called Explorer I.

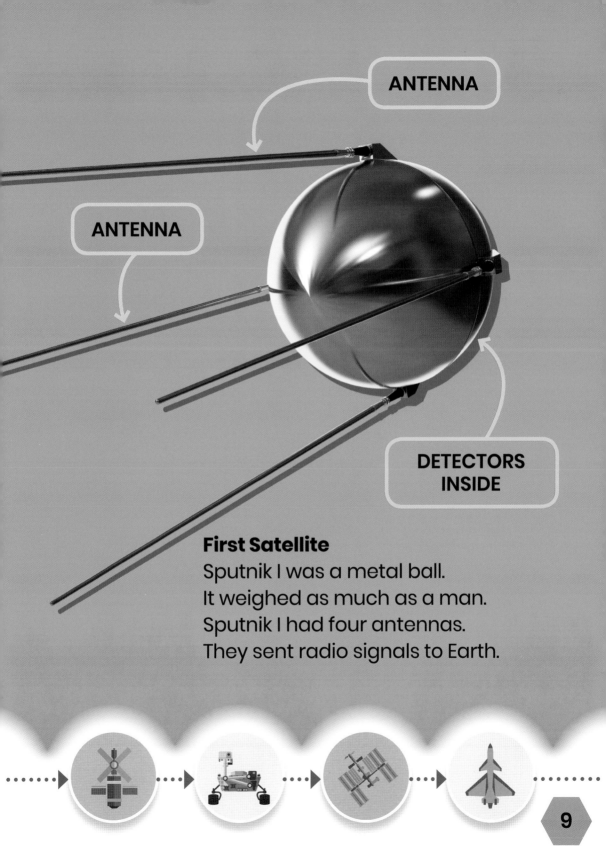

ANTENNA

ANTENNA

DETECTORS INSIDE

First Satellite
Sputnik I was a metal ball.
It weighed as much as a man.
Sputnik I had four antennas.
They sent radio signals to Earth.

Vostok I

Vostok I took the first human into space. His name was Yuri Gagarin. Vostok I flew for just 15 minutes. It orbited Earth once. Then, it came down fast. When it was near Earth, Gagarin jumped out wearing a parachute.

NASA
The United States set up a space agency. It was called NASA. Alan Shepard was the first American in space. He rode in a rocket named Freedom 7.

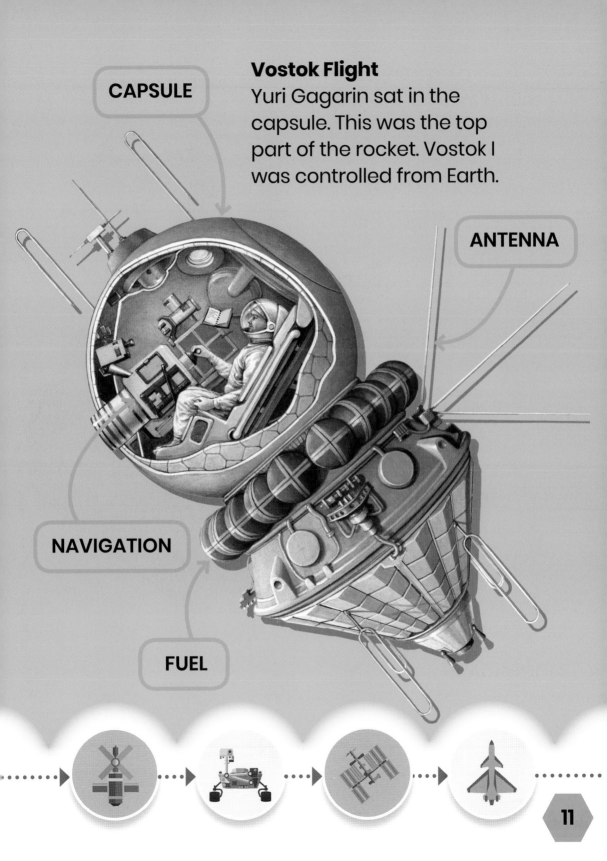

CAPSULE

Vostok Flight
Yuri Gagarin sat in the capsule. This was the top part of the rocket. Vostok I was controlled from Earth.

ANTENNA

NAVIGATION

FUEL

Apollo 11

Apollo 11 was a NASA spaceflight. It took the first humans to the Moon. There were three astronauts onboard. They traveled on a 950,000-mile (1,529,000-kilometers) round-trip!

Moonwalk
The lunar module landed on the Moon. Then, Neil Armstrong and Buzz Aldrin walked on the surface. They were the first people to do so. They picked up rock samples to study.

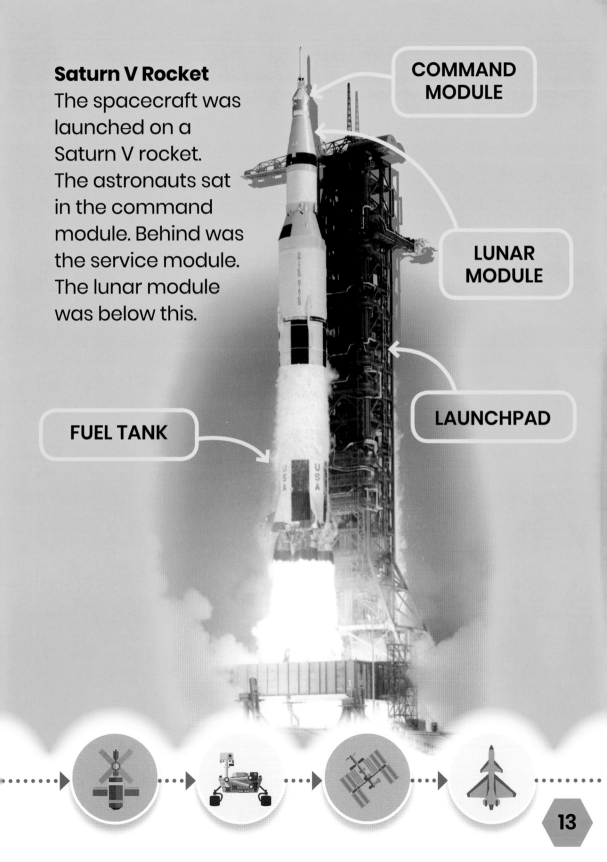

Saturn V Rocket
The spacecraft was launched on a Saturn V rocket. The astronauts sat in the command module. Behind was the service module. The lunar module was below this.

COMMAND MODULE

LUNAR MODULE

LAUNCHPAD

FUEL TANK

Skylab

Skylab was the first NASA space station. The crew flew there on a command module. They lived on Skylab for six months. They did experiments. Then, they flew back to Earth.

Space Suits

Space suits help astronauts survive in space. They give them oxygen to breathe. They keep them from getting too hot or cold.

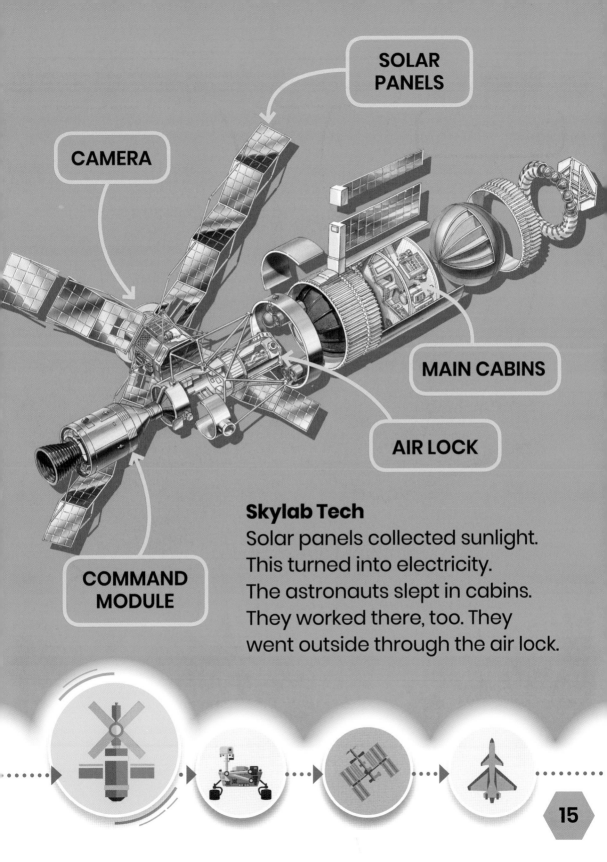

SOLAR PANELS

CAMERA

MAIN CABINS

AIR LOCK

COMMAND MODULE

Skylab Tech
Solar panels collected sunlight.
This turned into electricity.
The astronauts slept in cabins.
They worked there, too. They
went outside through the air lock.

Mars Rover

Scientists wanted to study Mars. They wanted to know if anything had lived there. They sent spacecraft called rovers to visit the planet.

Looking at Planets
Scientists sent Voyager probes to fly around Jupiter, Saturn, Uranus, and Neptune. Their cameras took pictures. They found amazing volcanoes.

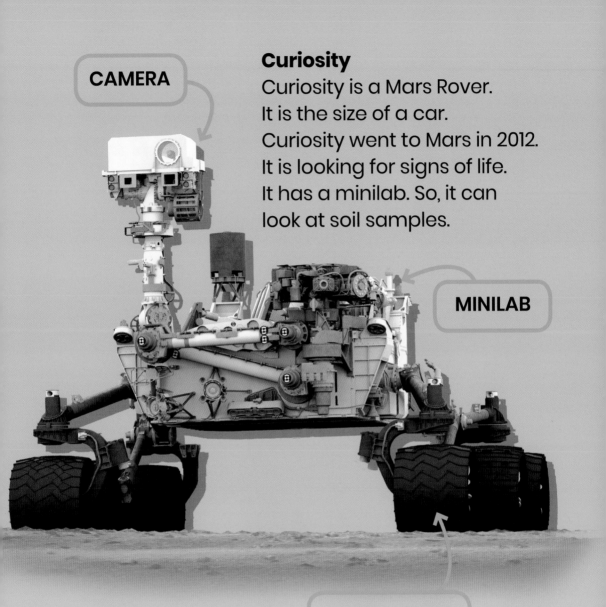

CAMERA

Curiosity

Curiosity is a Mars Rover.
It is the size of a car.
Curiosity went to Mars in 2012.
It is looking for signs of life.
It has a minilab. So, it can
look at soil samples.

MINILAB

STURDY TIRES

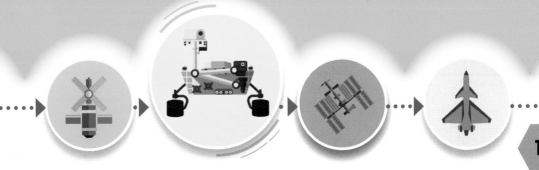

International Space Station

The International Space Station, or ISS, is a huge spacecraft. Astronauts live on board. They learn about living in space. There is no gravity. The crew float in the air!

Living in Space
The astronauts come from different countries. They work together in the space station. They live there for about six months. The crew do lots of experiments.

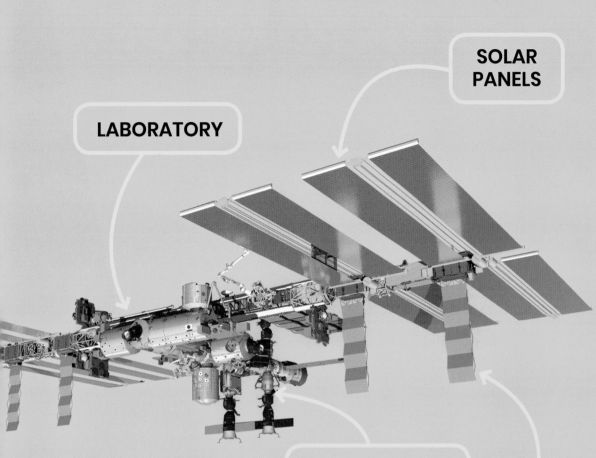

SOLAR PANELS

LABORATORY

LANDING DOCK

RADIATORS

Made in Space

The ISS was built in space. The crew put the parts together on space walks. Astronauts board from the dock. Radiators release heat to keep the ISS cool.

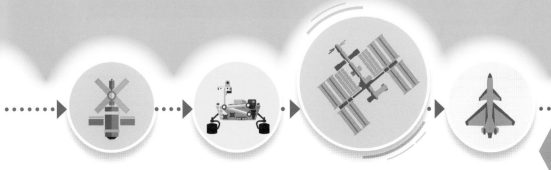

Future Space Travel

New spacecraft are being built. Some may take humans to Mars. People may live there in a space colony. What do you think spacecraft will do next?

Space Colony

People may set up a space colony on Mars. They will take water from the soil. They will grow food in a big greenhouse. They will need to get oxygen.

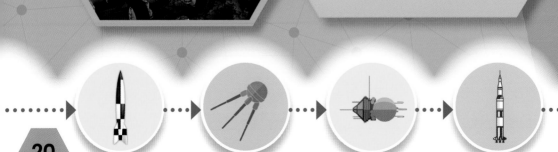

Orion Spacecraft

Astronauts may go to Mars by the 2030s. They will travel on the Orion. It will take a long time. People will need to stay healthy. They will have to take lots of supplies!

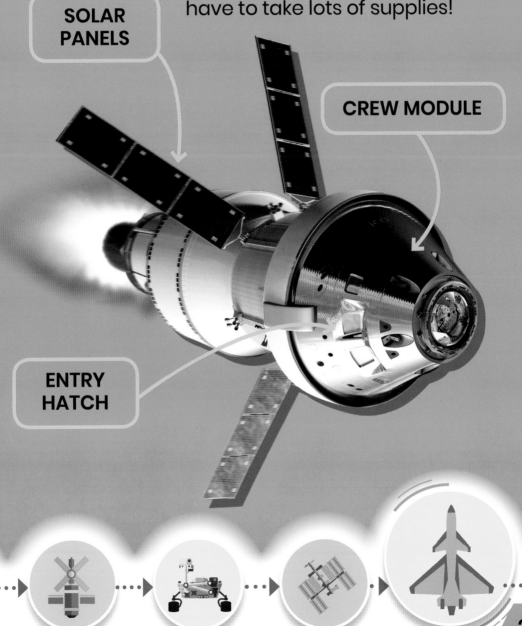

SOLAR PANELS

CREW MODULE

ENTRY HATCH

Timeline

600s	Fireworks are invented in China.
1232	The Chinese invent fire arrows. They use early gunpowder.
1944	The first V-2 rocket flies.
1949	Albert II, a monkey, rides in a V-2 rocket.
1957	Sputnik I is the first satellite in space.
1958	Explorer I is the first US satellite.
1958	NASA, the US space agency, is set up.
1961	Yuri Gagarin is the first human in space.
1969	Apollo 11 brings the first humans to the Moon. They walk on the surface.
1973	Skylab—the first US space station—launches.
1979	Voyagers 1 and 2 orbit Jupiter.
1980s	Voyagers 1 and 2 reach Saturn, Neptune, and Uranus.
1997	The first Mars rover, Sojourner, lands on the planet.
1998	The International Space Station launches into space.
2012	The Mars rover, Curiosity, reaches Mars.

Glossary

Apollo 11 A spacecraft that took the first humans to the Moon.

antenna A rod that sends radio signals. It also receives them.

astronaut Someone who travels to outer space or in a space station.

gravity The force that keeps objects and humans on Earth, instead of floating in air.

liquid fuel A fuel that mixes gases with liquid to make an explosion.

lunar module A small spacecraft that flies between a rocket and the Moon.

NASA The US agency that plans space missions and builds rockets.

orbit A path around an object, or to take such a path.

satellite A machine sent into space. It orbits Earth and sends signals back.

solar panel A panel that absorbs the Sun's rays. Then, it makes electricity from them.

Soviet Union A former country in Europe and Asia. It included Russia and other countries.

space suit A suit that keeps an astronaut alive in space.

Further Resources

Books

National Geographic Kids Ultimate Space Atlas Carolyn DeCristofano, National Geographic Kids, 2017

The Planets Heather Couper and Robert Dinwiddie, Dorling Kindersley, 2015

Websites

Discover cool facts about space from National Geographic: www.natgeokids.com/uk/?s=space

Find out all about space travel from NASA's Kids Club: www.nasa.gov/kidsclub/index.html

Index